...And He Shall Give Thee

the Desires of

Your Heart...

by

Jerry S. Baird

INTRODUCTION

Have you ever felt that you're never in the right place at the right time? Like, if you had been there five minutes earlier or five minutes later you would have been the one who won the jackpot, met the handsome man or the beautiful woman, got the best job, or whatever it is that makes you feel left out? Do you feel like all the good things happen to someone else? Do you ever feel like other Christians are more blessed than you are? Allow me to let you in on a secret of life: Celebrate what God has done for you. Permit yourself to commit your life to Him. And when He answers your prayers, write down what He did for you and thank Him for those answers first, before you present any of your problems or requests to Him. It is then that you will see what amazing things He will do for you.

If there has been a theme to my life as a Christian, it has been Psalm 37:4:

Delight thyself also in the Lord: and he shall give thee the desires of thine heart.

Isaiah 58:14 says it a little differently:

Then shalt thou delight thyself in the Lord; and I will cause thee to ride upon the high places of the earth, and feed thee with the heritage of Jacob thy father: for the mouth of the Lord hath spoken it.

Another scripture I would like to mention, because it has also been true in my life, is this:

Proverbs 3:6

In all thy ways acknowledge him, and he shall direct thy paths.

It has been my experience that God has, on various and sundry occasions, plucked desires from my heart that I could have never dreamed would be mine; then He handed them to me when I least expected them. Each desire was separate and distinct from all the other desires. Sometimes He just took a situation, turned it around, and made me blessed. These experiences have been strength for me down through the years. They demonstrate that, not only does God hear the words of my mouth, **He reads my heart and directs my path.**

Acts 14:27 tells us this:

And when they were come, and had gathered the church together, they <u>rehearsed</u> all that God had done with them, and how he had opened the door of faith unto the Gentiles.

For years I have shared the following stories with my daughters about when God gave me the desires of my heart. I've also included a couple stories about people to whom God gave them the desires of *their* heart. Now I am putting them in book form for my children and my grandchildren to keep and read and <u>rehearse</u> to their children, and for others to read.

I hope that they, in turn, will write down what God has done for them; and that they, too, will experience God giving them the desires of their heart.

And, I hope you, also, will experience the pure delight of having God give you the desires of *your* heart.

When He does, *rehearse* it in the ears of your loved ones.

Jerry S. Baird

Acknowledgements

My heartfelt thanks to

my daughter Becky Pierce for all her

encouragement,

and to

my daughter Rachel Johnson

and

Amber Pantoja

for proofreading this book.

Table of Contents

The Mirror

When I first became a Christian, I was very worried about graven images. I had read Exodus 20:4 (King James Version and part of the Ten Commandments) which says:

> 4: *Thou shalt not make unto thee any graven image, or any likeness of anything that is in heaven above, or that is in the earth beneath, or that is in the water under the earth.*

This was serious business. So, even though I loved ceramics and such things, I tried to be very careful not to offend the Lord.

Well, one day, in the drugstore where I bought my lunch each day, there was a lovely little mirror. It wasn't very big. The stand for the mirror had three legs, was sort of ornate pewter, and was maybe three or four inches tall, at the most. The mirror itself was oval and about two inches in height and was framed by two cute little, darling, adorable cherubs on each side. I loved that mirror and wanted it so badly. My tormented eyes looked longingly at it each day.

Finally the clerk said, "Why don't you buy it?" I don't recall what answer I gave her, but it was probably incomprehensible.

One day I went to pay my lunch bill and the little mirror was gone. Soon I forgot about it.

The year rolled by and soon it was Christmas. Our family had a good friend named Jeannie who lived down the street from us. We hadn't exchanged gifts with Jeannie in years; but this particular year she decided to buy gifts for all of us. On Christmas morning everyone had opened their gift from Jeannie except Mom and me. Mom opened her gift first, and there was the little mirror!

I said, "That isn't yours. It's mine!"

She said, "No it isn't. Jeannie gave it to me."

"Well, Jeannie made a mistake."

"No she didn't. My name is on the package."

"Oka-a-a-y, I will open this gift in front of me, and it will be unmistakably for you!"

2

And sure enough, in the package with my name on it was a petticoat (A petticoat is a full slip that was worn under dresses. We used to wear such things in those days.) And it was about four sizes larger than what I was wearing—in those days. There was no doubt that the petticoat was for Mom.

"Now," I said, "we are going to call Jeannie and ask her what she gave to you and what she gave to me. And don't be trying to send her any signals about you wanting that mirror!"

So we called Jeannie and she confirmed what I already knew: The petticoat was Mom's, and the mirror was MINE!

"How did you know the mirror was yours?" Mom asked.

So I told her about the little mirror at the drugstore and how much I wanted it but was afraid that I might be offending God if I bought it.

We looked at each other and wondered out loud, "How does it happen that Jeannie bought that exact mirror?" We called Jeannie and said, "Jeannie, would come over to our house and tell us how you happened to buy that particular mirror?"

Jeanie only lived about four doors down the street and she was at our house in about five minutes; and this is what she said:

"I felt very strongly that I wanted to buy gifts for all of you this year, so Harold (her husband) and I went to White Front (one of the first discount stores in California) and started looking for gifts for all of you. We found gifts for everyone except Jerry. It was getting late and just about time for the store to close, but we couldn't find anything that seemed right for her, so we left. Suddenly, I knew I had to go back into the store, and we rushed in just before they closed the doors. We went from counter to counter and couldn't find anything; then something said, 'Jerry.' We stopped in our tracks and looked at the counter in front of us, and there was this mirror. We knew instantly it was the right gift and we bought it. I guess I just got the packages mixed up and put the wrong name on her package. But the mirror is for Jerry!"

She, also, wanted to know how I knew it was for me. So we told her about the mirror at the drugstore and how much I wanted it but was afraid to buy it.

God had given me the desire of my heart!

Peppermint Ice Cream

I've never been a big ice cream fan, but sometimes the thought of eating a certain food will stick in my mind and I'll crave things like liver and onions, sauerkraut, or anything with lemon, tart or sour foods with a bite, etc. Anyway, you get the idea. Well, this one day I went to lunch across the street from where I was working. I ate my lunch at the drug store on the corner (the same drug store with the mirror). When I finished my lunch, all of a sudden I really wanted some peppermint ice cream! I don't know where that thought came from; because, like I said, I've never been a big ice cream fan, and we never kept ice cream at the house. But, nevertheless, I asked the waitress if they had peppermint ice cream.

"I don't think so," she said, "but I'll ask the chef. Pretty soon she came back and said, "No, I'm sorry, but we don't have any peppermint ice cream."

As I recall, they had the usual chocolate, strawberry and vanilla. "No," I said, "I want peppermint, but thanks for checking." I went back to work and forgot all about peppermint ice cream.

When I got home from work that evening, my mom said, "Look what I bought today. Would you like to try some?"

I looked at what she was holding up. It was a quart of peppermint ice cream! I said, "How did you happen to buy peppermint ice cream?"

She said, "I don't know. I just saw it in the store and it looked like it would taste good! Do you want some?"

Do birds fly? When I told her about me asking for it at the drug store lunch counter we were both amazed.

God had given me the desire of my heart.

The Cigarette

It was a rainy day and I was attempting to cross a very busy intersection in Los Angeles, California. Even though I had become a Christian, I was still puffing away at cigarettes, and the rain was getting my cigarette all wet.

I looked around and saw a little lady with an umbrella heading my way. I thought, "I wish she'd offer to share her umbrella with me." When she got up to me she said, "Would you like to share my umbrella?" I thought, "Wow! That's awesome!" By then, my cigarette was really getting soggy. Soggy cigarettes stink, in case you didn't know. And I said, "Yes, thank you. I would like that very much."

As we were crossing the street, the little woman asked, "Do you know Jesus as your Savior?" I'm quite sure she was expecting me to say "No." But I replied, "Yes." My cigarette was beginning to feel like it weighed five pounds at that point. "I know it doesn't look like it, but I am trying to quit. It's just that I throw the pack of cigarettes away and then drive as fast as I can to the nearest liquor store to buy another pack." By this time my cigarette was so soggy I just dropped it on the street and ground it out with my shoe. We stepped up on the curb on the other side of the street and the lady said, "I will pray for God to help you quit." I thanked her both for offering to share her umbrella and for offering to pray for me, and we said goodbye.

Now, I was someone who really enjoyed smoking. I liked the smell, the taste, and the very act of smoking (unless it was wet and stinky). So this was not going to be an easy task. The thought of quitting was pretty far out there. But I knew it wasn't pleasing to God and that my body is the temple of God; so, the cigarettes were going to have to go.

One day, not too long after meeting the lady with the umbrella in the rain, I was having coffee with someone I really admired. We were smoking and talking and the ash on the end of my cigarette got really long. I held the cigarette over the ashtray to flick it, and how I missed that ashtray I will never know; but those ashes went everywhere. It was the biggest mess, and I was so embarrassed. I couldn't even do a decent job of cleaning it up. But from that moment on, I began to wonder why I even wanted to be involved with such a dirty habit.

The Lord had made it hateful in my eyes, and soon after that, I quit smoking.

When my father realized that I had quit smoking, he asked me why I was quitting. I explained that, as a Christian, I didn't feel it should be part of my life (I am paraphrasing.). So each day he would ask me, "Have you had a smoke today?" I would answer no, and he would toss his cigarette pack on the coffee table or whatever table was near. "Here's some smokes, if you want them." Well, I didn't want them. But one day, after I had gone without cigarettes for about a month, I thought, "You know, I should reward myself." I reached for a cigarette (There were always plenty of cigarettes lying around the house.) and I lit up. And when I did, a scripture and a vision immediately came to me. And this is what they were:

> *Behold, I will make thee a new*
> *sharp threshing instrument having*
> *teeth: thou shalt thresh the mountains,*
> *and beat them small, and shalt make*
> *the hills as chaff. Isaiah 41:15*

That's a great and inspiring scripture. There was a problem; however, because in the vision I saw about the sharp threshing instrument having teeth—all the teeth had cigarette butts stuck in-between them and the instrument couldn't thresh! I put the cigarette out and I never smoked again. And that's been over 50 years ago.

God had given me the desire of my heart and helped me quit smoking!

The Office Cleaning Woman

I worked for a long time in an insurance broker's office in Los Angeles, California. I usually came in early and stayed late. One evening, just shortly after Christmas, I was just closing up my desk when a very frail young woman came in and wanted to know if it was okay if she started cleaning up the office. I said, "Of course, come right in." So she began dusting and cleaning the office. I asked her what her name was and told her my name was Jerry. She said her name was Gigi. I followed up with, "Did you have a nice Christmas?"

Gigi stopped working and looked me square in the eye. "I wouldn't have said anything, if you hadn't asked, but, no, I didn't have a nice Christmas. While all of you were having Thanksgiving and Christmas together, I was alone—alone, waiting for your holidays to be over."

I don't think I need to tell you that I wished I had kept my mouth shut. "I'm so sorry," I said. "I didn't mean to offend you."

"That's okay," she said. "I'm used to it. But I've never had a birthday party—or a birthday gift. In fact, I have never been given a gift in my life.   And while all of you are celebrating, I am alone.   I have always been alone."

Well, I was properly horrified at everything Gigi said to me. As I was driving home from work that evening, I wondered what I could do for someone like her.   Then it occurred to me that I had one ceramic left over from Christmas gifts I had given to the girls in my Sunday school class.   They were lovely ceramics of little ladies in full dresses—and I still had the box it came in. So when I got home, I put the ceramic lady in the box, gift-wrapped it, put Gigi's name on it and set it out so I would not forget to take it to work in the morning.

The next morning I got to work early, put the box in a file cabinet so people wouldn't be asking questions, and waited for the end of the day. When the work day was finished and the office had emptied, I put the box with Gigi's name on it in the center of my desk and left the office.

The next morning there was a note and a little red Bible on my desk. Some of you will be too young to remember the little red Bibles. They were popular for a while. They were about one inch square and the entire Bible was printed in them—Old and New Testaments. They were really quite amazing. In the note, she thanked me profusely and said she had actually been given a gift and it was the little red Bible. She wanted me to have it.

I didn't see Gigi for quite a while after that; but one afternoon she came in early to make sure our paths crossed. She wanted to know if I would pray with her. I said I would. My employer had left for the day and there was a carpet in his office, so we knelt down by the couch in his office. This is what she said she wanted to pray about:

"I want you to pray with me to ask God if he will allow me to die. I don't want to live any more. I don't intend to kill myself, but I just want Him to take me home."

Gigi had some sort of disease that caused her to have a strangling situation in her throat. It required that she exercise several times a day to keep from strangling, and she was very exhausted. So we prayed, first for God to heal her, and second, if He wasn't going to heal her, to take her home.

13

I never saw her again. One week went by; no Gigi. Two weeks went by; no Gigi. I kept asking the other janitors about her. They said she was sick. Finally I went to the office of the building and told them of my concerns and told them that Gigi was very frail. If she was sick for that long, then she was in big trouble. The office staff thanked me and told me they would look into it. Some time went by, and then the manager of the office of the building caught up with me and told me that they had found her in the city morgue. She had died in a public bathroom. The problem she was having with her throat had killed her.

The staff in the office of the building was so touched by her circumstances that they went to her funeral. They said no one came to her funeral except her brother, and he didn't seem to even want to be there. The office manager said that it was very sad. There was not one other person on the face of this earth that cared whether Gigi lived or died.

But God cared, and He gave her the desire of her heart. I am so glad that her life touched mine. I look forward to seeing her in Heaven.

The Office of the Building

My life was greatly enriched by my meeting Gigi. I met all the janitors, and they knew everything that was going on in the business building, and, as I recall, there were four or five stories to that building. So anytime my employer wanted to know what was going on in the building, he asked me.

One day, Mr. C. (the company CEO) stepped to his office door and asked Mr. H. (the company treasurer) to come into his office. They stood at his window looking down at something, gesturing a lot and scratching their heads. Finally they said, "Let's ask Jerry." So, they called me to the window and pointed down to some new construction. They had asked everyone they knew what was going up, but no one knew. Mr. C. said, "Jerry, you don't happen to know what is going down there, do you?"

Now it just so happened that the people in the office of the building, just a few days earlier, had told me they knew what was going on there and that they had the architect's renderings and that I was free to look at them anytime. So I pretended to study the view out Mr. C.'s window and said, "Now, as I understand it, you want to know what that ramp is for, and you want to know what they are building. Is that correct?"

"Yes!" they both said. "You *know*, don't you?"

"Give me five minutes. I'll be right back."

So I went to the office of the building and told them about my employer's interest in the new construction next door. Well, they loaded me up with the architect's drawings, the name of the place that was being built, and a bunch of other stuff that I can't remember at this late date. They even gave me a picture of the building our office was in when it was built about 25 years earlier.

When I came walking into Mr. C.'s office with all that information, he just shook his head. "How do you do that?" he asked.

So I went over to the window, pointed to the ramp they were trying to figure out and said, "That leads to the parking garage that is being built. To the left is going to be a swimming pool. And the rest of it will be a hotel, and I told him the name of the hotel.

"Now," I said, "you two look at that as long as you want to, but I have to take it all back." And I left them there shaking their heads and pondering all the information I had given them.

I never told them about Gigi, so they didn't have a clue. But even for the very brief time that I knew Gigi, she blessed my life.

Proverbs 3:6

In all thy ways acknowledge him, and he shall direct thy paths.

Meeting My Husband-to-Be

My life seemed pretty humdrum compared to other people, like my Aunt Margaret. She was very pretty and had been a model and her pictures had been in popular magazines. When she got married, she married a handsome naval officer who later left the Navy and became an optometrist. They settled down and belonged to the local country club, had three adorable children and lived the good life. When their children got older, her oldest son became an official candidate for the Naval Academy in Annapolis, Maryland, and ultimately he became a midshipman at the Naval Academy. I really envied and admired my aunt and her family, but I was certain that none of that was going to be my lot in life. (Hold on to that thought.)

Before I was married, I worked in Los Angeles a long time. I liked to go out for lunch instead of bringing my lunch to work; so, I would try every eating place near to my work. Finally, I had eaten at every place near enough to the office to walk to, and I was on the search for a new place to eat lunch. One day, not wanting to eat at all the old familiar places, I asked my boss if he knew of any place nearby that I could try. And he said yes! I couldn't believe my ears.

"You do," I asked incredulously.

"Yes," he said. "You have to try this place. It's just across the street."

"Across the street? I've tried every place near here. I don't remember any restaurants across the street."

"It's a little, tiny place next to some kind of lender. If you blinked your eyes you would miss it."

"Is the food good?"

"Never mind the food. It's worth the price of admission to go there! An old man and old woman run it, and it's like a "Punch and Judy" show." ("Punch and Judy" was a puppet show where the puppets hit each other on the head a lot.).

"The wife is the waitress and the husband is the short-order cook. They have a parking lot out back; so, in between orders, he runs out and parks cars. They are yelling at each other all the time. Go over and try it at least once."

My interest was piqued. I had to try that place; so the next day I crossed the street and went down as far as the lenders' storefront. Sure enough, next door to it was a little, tiny restaurant. I entered and looked around for a place to sit down. Now, it wasn't as if there were myriads of places to sit: All the seats were at a horse-shoe shaped counter. I picked a place nearest to the window where the waitress would give her food orders to the cook (when he wasn't parking cars).

Mimi, the waitress, (the old woman) came over and asked me what I would like to order.

I said I would like to see a menu. Well, they didn't have a menu. She said she would tell me what they had to eat. In reality, she *told* me *what* to eat; and, as I recall, it was an eggplant and tomato dish. I obediently ate it and asked for my check, as it was time to go back to work.

"How did you like it?" she asked.

"Oh, it was delicious, thank you."

"Was there anything wrong with it?"

"No, I loved it, really!"

"Do you want anything else to eat?"

"No, thank you. I have to go back to work or I'll be late."

Her next question was, "Would like anything else? How about some cigarettes?"

I declined and said no thank you.

"Don't we have the brand you smoke?" she asked.

I said, "I don't smoke."

"You don't smoke!?" This was more than she could wrap her brain around; everyone she knew smoked. There had to be something wrong with her selection of cigarettes.

"No, really, you have a fine selection of cigarettes. I just don't smoke."

"You don't smoke!" she exclaimed in disbelief. "You must be a very good girl!"

Well, that launched my association with Joe and Mimi. Every time I went over there it was something new: everything from trying to fix me up with the boys at the lending place next door to bragging to the customers about what a good girl I was; "AND," she would proclaim for all the customers to hear, "SHE DOESN'T EVEN SMOKE!"

Eventually, I was looking for another place to eat and stopped going to Joe and Mimi's. Time went by. One day I was crossing the street and I met Mimi in the middle of the street, and asked, "How's everything going at the restaurant?"

"Well, we don't have the restaurant anymore. We sold it and the parking lot and bought a parking lot across the street." She pointed to a parking lot on the corner across from where we were standing. "You work in that big building right there," she said, pointing to the building where I worked. "You should park your car on our lot."

"Yes, I do work in that building, and I'll think about it," I said. Then we each went our separate ways and I didn't see her for a long time. But one day we met again crossing the street, and I asked her again how she was and how Joe was. She said that Joe had had a terrible heart attack and that they didn't expect him to live. She said if he did live he would be bed-ridden and not even be able to sit up for the rest of his life!

I was properly horrified at that. This encounter was on a Wednesday, and I always went to church on Wednesdays, so I told her I would ask for prayer for Joe. Mimi was flabbergasted. She had never had anyone offer to pray for them before. So that night, at prayer meeting, I asked for prayer for Joe. Once again I forgot about them.

Sometime later, Mimi and I met as we were crossing the street again.

"Hi, Mimi," I said. "How's Joe?"

"Don't you know?" she said. "You prayed for him!"

I was not expecting that answer and had no idea what kind of impact my offering to have prayer for Joe had on her.

"No, Mimi, I don't know. Tell me."

"Well," she continued, "Joe was lying in the hospital bed thinking he would never sit up again, much less walk again, when a man in a white outfit walked over to his bed and told him to rise up and walk."

I said, "What did Joe do?"

"Well, he told the man what the doctor said about his condition."

"What did the man in white say?"

"The man in white touched him and told him he was healed and to rise up and walk."

"What did Joe do?"

"He got up and walked all over the room! Later, when the doctor came in the room, Joe was sitting up in his bed."

"What did the doctor say?"

"He said, 'Why are you sitting up?' He told Joe that he would never do more than sit up."

"What did Joe say?"

"Joe told him about the man in white and that he said Joe was healed."

"What did the doctor say?"

"He said Joe would never walk again."

"What did Joe say to that?"

"Joe got out of bed and walked around the room."

"What did the doctor say?"

"The doctor examined Joe and told him he was going to let him go home, that he was healed!"

Okay, my head was about to explode after she told me all that.

She said, "Joe can't even talk about it without crying. You've got to come and talk to him."

As you can imagine, I had to see Joe, and I told Mimi I would come over to their parking lot when I got off work. I thought about that for the rest of the day. And at the end of the day I closed my desk and headed for their parking lot.

We talked for a long time, and finally it was getting pretty late and I said I had to go.

"Jerry, why don't you park your car on our lot?" Mimi said.

I had to think about that one. There was also a parking lot right next to the building where I worked, and the boy that parked cars there had a crush on me and let me park for free. And, of course, free parking is always better than paying for it! I explained to them about parking for free, but I promised that if anything ever happened to that free parking space, I would come and park on their parking lot.

That all happened on a Wednesday, and as you know, I went to church on Wednesday nights. That night they were taking prayer requests at church and I told them about the opportunity I had to witness to Joe and Mimi and that I had this free parking space, and I asked them to pray about it with me, which they did.

The next day my car was parked for free, as usual, and I went to work. When I got off work that night there was an 8-1/2" x 11" piece of paper with a note on it under my windshield wiper. It read: "This is not a free parking lot. If you want to continue to park here, please stop in at the office and we will make arrangements for you to park and tell you how much it will cost. The Management."

I was shocked; but I had publicly put that before the Lord and this was the answer. So I drove across the street to Joe and Mimi's parking lot and told them what happened. And even though I would have preferred to get free parking, I was amazed at how quickly my prayer was answered.

Once I started parking on Joe and Mimi's parking lot, I spent a lot of time after work talking to them about the Lord. One day they had a story to tell me:

A friend of theirs lived in a hotel that adjoined their parking lot. As long as they could remember, their friend had to walk with crutches. But on this day, she walked over to them without the crutches.

"What happened?" they asked. "How does it happen that you aren't walking with your crutches?"

The friend then told them this surprising story: She had been sitting in one of the lounge seats at the hotel where she lived, and she was listening to a conversation that two young men were having who were sitting behind her. She wasn't trying to eavesdrop, but she couldn't help hearing them as they talked about Jesus. Finally, she interrupted them and asked them if Jesus could heal her. She said one of the young men looked her directly in the eye and said, "Yes He can, Mother. Would you allow us to pray for you?" Well, of course she did and then she went back to her room—on her crutches. So much for healing—or so she thought.

That night, when she went to bed, she placed her crutches at the foot of her bed like she always did, and then she settled in to go to sleep. Later that night she needed to get up and go to the bathroom. As she started to get up, she accidentally kicked her crutches off the end of the bed and out of reach. "Oh, no," she said, "what will I do?" At that point, she heard a voice say, "Get up and walk!"

"What did you do?" Joe and Mimi asked.

"I got up and walked, and I haven't needed my crutches ever since!"

Well, you can imagine, especially after Joe's healing, the interest that Joe and Mimi had, and we talked about it a lot. This was all very fascinating, and I would tell the people at church each Wednesday the latest episode with Joe and Mimi.

One day I came to the parking lot after work and Mimi could hardly wait for me to get there.

"We met your husband today! Can we give him your phone number?" Well, that was a surprise, especially since I wasn't married and never had been.

"All the good ones are getting away, Jerry. Please let us give him your phone number." So I said okay. I couldn't argue with that.

After a day or so, I got a phone call from someone who said his name was Bob and that Joe and Mimi had given him my phone number and would I like to go out for coffee. I was a little nervous about that, because I had been on blind dates before, and I really didn't know what to expect. I'm sure Bob felt the same way. But what a surprise I was in for. When we met I could hardly speak. He was the cutest naval officer you'd ever want to see.

Our next date was to be a picnic, and I spent a lot of money buying just the right picnic basket, cooking Cornish hens, making Waldorf salad, and some other stuff I can't remember.

It was beautiful! We were going to drive to San Diego and have lunch by the ocean.

Now, I had lived in Southern California most of my life, and most of the time the weather was pretty mild—especially in San Diego. But on that day, I have to tell you, I think the temperature dropped 40 degrees—at least, that's how it felt. When we got out of the car and headed for a table and benches, I thought I would freeze to death; but I was determined to make the best of it. This lunch had cost me a lot of money and time and we were going to eat it!

A lot of people make their Waldorf salad with mayonnaise, but, as I recall, I used whipping cream. The whipped cream fell and looked like something really disgusting. The Cornish hens were cold. And it was just too freezing cold out there to eat that picnic lunch. I was shivering so bad my teeth were chattering.

Bob was very sweet about it, and it was pretty funny when you think about it. We laughed about it over the years. So I lived through that and we toured around the rest of the day. At the end of the day he said he had a wonderful time and did I want to go out again. And, yes, I did want to go out again, but I never tried to make Waldorf salad again—ever! I don't think I ever made Cornish hens again, either.

To make a long story short, Bob and I got married and ultimately moved to the Naval Academy in Annapolis, Maryland, where Bob was assigned, and my life was changed forever.

Did you catch the part about Bob being a naval officer and that we lived at the Naval Academy?

Once again the Lord had plucked a desire from deep within my heart and handed it to me. I serve a Risen Savior!

Rhubarb Pie

I have always loved rhubarb. Rhubarb grows in stalks, sort of like celery only it's red and not green, and the plant is much bigger. As a little girl I would take a stalk of it and eat it uncooked. For me it was just a wonderful, tart treat.

When I was in grammar school, I would walk to school. On my way to school, there was a huge rhubarb plant in front of one of the houses I would pass. I would walk past it again on my way home. When I got to that house, I would look all around. If no one was looking, I would break off a big stalk of rhubarb and run as fast as I could. When I was out of sight of the owner of the rhubarb plant, I would brush all the dirt off my prized rhubarb stalk and eat it all the way home. It was dee-licious!

As I grew older, I loved rhubarb pie. Sometimes I had to settle for strawberry-rhubarb pie, because not that many people can deal with just straight rhubarb.

Well, one day, soon after I was married, I got hungry for rhubarb. Fortunately, it was in season. So when I got off work I stopped at the market on the way home and bought some. Thoughts of a bowl of cooked rhubarb danced in my head. When I got home, I went straight to the kitchen and started cooking.

My husband came in and said, "What are you doing?"

I said, "I'm making rhubarb."

"Rhubarb? You like rhubarb?"

"Yes, I do. Here taste this. See if it tastes right to you."

Now, I didn't know it at the time, but my husband always wanted to be a cook. So he began to experiment—with *my* rhubarb!

"Hmmmm. What this needs is more sugar." So he put in more sugar. Then I tasted it.

"Well, now, you've diluted the taste. Put more cinnamon in it."

Then he tasted it. "Have you ever tried allspice in it?" So we put in allspice.

To make a short story long would be to add all the details of what else went into that rhubarb. Let's just say that, if we had eaten any more of it, it probably would have melted the enamel off our teeth. So we threw the rest of it away.

This happened on a Wednesday night, and, as you know, on Wednesday nights we had mid-week church meetings. So we cleaned up the dishes and started to get ready for church. I didn't really want to go, because we had an interim pastor who only talked about himself, and I had heard all I wanted to hear about him. So I said, "You go ahead. I don't think I want to go." It took quite a bit of persuading, but eventually I agreed that I shouldn't stay home and I reluctantly got ready to go.

The sermon was exactly what I thought it would be: it was all about him. I was bummed that I had come. After church, I was just standing around waiting for my husband to say let's leave.

As I was standing there, one of the elderly ladies in the church came up to me and said, "Sister Jerry, I did something that I've never done before. I hope you won't think I'm crazy!"

I said, "What did you do?"

She said, "Well, I've never done anything like this before."

"Well, what did you do?"

"Well," she began, "I was working around the house and my husband was in the back yard. As I was getting some house work done, the Lord spoke to me and said, *'Why don't you bake a rhubarb pie for Sister Jerry?'* I said, *'I can't do that, Lord; she'll think I'm crazy.'* So I just kept doing my house work, and pretty soon the Lord spoke to me again: *'Why don't you bake a rhubarb pie for Sister Jerry?'* And I said, *'No, Lord, she'll think I'm crazy.'* So I just kept doing my housework. Pretty soon my husband came in from the backyard and said he needed some things at the store. So we went to the store. At the store he was going here and there picking up things. I wanted some things, so we agreed to meet at the produce department. I was walking around the produce department trying to decide which fruits and vegetables I needed when my husband walked up. He said, *'Hey, look, they have fresh rhubarb. Why don't you bake Sister Jerry a rhubarb pie?'* Well, I knew when I was whipped, so we bought the rhubarb and went home. Now I need for you to follow me out to my car."

I couldn't believe what I was hearing. As we started toward the foyer, I said, "Did you bake a *rhubarb* pie for me?"

"Yes, but I've never baked a rhubarb pie. I've never done anything like this before. I hope you don't think I'm crazy!"

She went out the front door of the church and held it open for me to pass. As I walked through the door and past her she said, "I've never baked a rhubarb pie before. I don't know whether you will like it. I don't know whether I did it right or not!"

The parking lot was emptying out as the Wednesday evening parishioners were leaving for home.

I said, "Really!! A *rhubarb* pie!!"

By the time we got to the car, the parking lot was half empty. She opened the car door and pulled out the most beautiful rhubarb pie I had ever seen. Somehow, she had poured rich, thick cream over the top crust and sprinkled sugar and cinnamon on it and baked it. It was fantastic!

"I hope you don't think I'm crazy," she said apologetically.

Then I explained to her how much I loved rhubarb pie and how we had destroyed the rhubarb I brought home and how much I wanted some rhubarb. But I don't think she heard me, because she just kept saying, "I've never done anything like this before!"

Bob had caught up with us while were talking about the rhubarb pie. He walked up to us and started to ask if I was ready to go home when he saw the pie.

"What's that?" he asked.

"That," I said, "is a RHUBARB pie! The **Lord** told her to make it for me!"

Some friends came home with us from church that night. We cut that rhubarb pie into four pieces and ate it all at one sitting.

God had given me the desire of my heart!

The Children

A while after the rhubarb pie experience, I discovered I was pregnant with our first daughter, Becky, and Bob had been assigned to the Naval Academy in Annapolis, Maryland. I was really sick all nine months, so I was assigned to the head of the GYN Department at the Naval Academy Hospital. I couldn't keep any food down and was hospitalized several times and given IV's to keep me from dehydrating. In short, I was given special treatment. So that I didn't have to wait at the doctor's office, because I was so sick, when I walked through the door in the doctors' office, my file was always put on the top of the pile of the other women's files, and I was taken ahead of everyone else.

Now, the head of the GYN Department was a really good-looking man, and all the women wanted him to be their doctor; but, this was a military hospital, and everyone had to take the doctor that was available. Everyone, that is, except me.

I would just have time to enter the building, sit down, and hear the women say, "Oh, I hope I can get Dr. _____ today." (I'm not going to say his name, because I have no way of knowing whether he is still alive.) And almost before the words were out of their mouth, the nurse would enter the room and say, "Doctor _____ will see you, Mrs. Baird."

There were quite a few wives of the men in Bob's department who were pregnant, and we always had group appointments; so the same people were always there.

"How do you do that?" they would moan. I would just smile, get up and go see the best looking doctor in the hospital. It didn't keep me from being sick and throwing up all day, but it made it a little easier.

We had a lot of trauma during my pregnancy, i.e., Bob's father died, Bob was hospitalized, I was hospitalized, etc., so the doctors assured me that all the nausea and vomiting I was experiencing would not happen if I got pregnant again; because they believed the nausea and vomiting was brought on by the trauma. So I got pregnant with our second daughter, Rachel. Trust me: I was just as sick with her. But this time I had a baby at home, so they didn't want to admit me to the hospital: I was treated as an out-patient. It was awful. I was so sick and nauseated and dizzy that it was hard to stand up and prepare food for Becky. Most of the time all I could do was lie on the couch and offer her crackers and milk. Her first word was "cracker." We finally had to have someone come in and take care of the baby and me. But the nine months, which seemed like nine years, were finally over and it was time to deliver that baby.

Autumn on the East Coast is a very beautiful time of the year. Since I grew up on the West Coast, the season changes were fascinating to me. I knew my mother was going to come to stay for a while after I had the baby, so I had a deep desire for the beautiful leaves to still be on the trees when she arrived. Also, I was really hoping that I would get the same doctor to deliver my second baby. Finally the day arrived for the baby to be born. The trees still looked glorious in all their color, but one good rain or strong wind and they would all be gone. Things weren't looking too hopeful about Mom seeing the beautiful fall foliage. When I got into the delivery room, they said this was my favorite doctor's night off and that a different doctor would be delivering my second baby. Bummer! I was disappointed, but, the baby was ready to be born: the time had come. When the doctor walked in—it was the head of the GYN Department! My favorite doctor! I was shocked.

I said, "They said you weren't on duty tonight! What happened?"

He said, "The other doctor wanted the night off and I said I would take his place."

I was still in the hospital when Mom arrived, so I had no idea about the leaves on the trees—in fact, I had forgotten about the leaves. But she had arrived in time. She said that, as they descended into the airport in Washington, D.C., the trees were ablaze with color.

Once again, the Lord gave me the desire of my heart, but this time it was a double header!

My Grandmother's Visit

When Becky and Rachel were very young, they both went to the daycare center on the base where Bob was stationed. I worked part-time, and this gave the girls a lot of children to play with.

One day, they came home with tickets to the circus and wanted to know if we could go. We thought about it and said yes. There would be a lot of animals there, and we thought it was something they would enjoy.

Well, it really wasn't that great, and after being there an hour or so, the girls wanted to know if we could go home. We said sure. So we all piled into the car and went home.

When we pulled into our carport, all of a sudden I could tell someone had been there.

I said, "Someone has been here."

Bob said, "How can you tell?"

"I can see where they walked up the sidewalk. I can see them at the door."

Bob got out of the car and examined the entire walk that lead up to the front door.

"There are no footprints here, Jerry."

"I know," I said, "but I can see someone go up to the door."

"Well, who was it?"

"I don't know."

We got the little girls out of the car and walked to the front door. Just as we got to the door, our phone began to ring. (Remember, we're still in the age of no cell phones.)

"We're going to find out who was here when we answer that phone call," I said.

So we opened the door and rushed to the phone before it quit ringing. It was my mother. She called to tell us that my grandmother had died.

Let me tell you about my Grandmother. She was a born-again, Holiness minister. She never set foot in a movie theatre, and she certainly would not have gone to a circus.

We missed a precious visit that day. It was a visit that I will always wonder how it would have gone. But I still carry in my heart that, nevertheless, she came to visit before she departed this earth.

It is a sweet memory, one that I will always cherish. I look forward to seeing her in Heaven.

The Puppet Ministry

Soon after Rachel was born, Bob's orders came through for him to go to California, so we found a nice home to rent in San Diego. Bob spend a lot of time at sea and I stayed home with the girls.   While he was at sea, I developed a lot of material for Children's Church at the church we were attending. Puppets were having a revival, and I had read about people using them in their ministries. This was just before "Sesame Street," the famous TV children's program, hit the airwaves.

I found a teacher's supply store nearby that sold puppets. There wasn't a big choice like there is today, so I bought a crow, a frog, a ventriloquist doll, and, if my memory serves me correctly, a farmer puppet. Armed with my new tools (puppets), I launched my puppet ministry in children's' church.

Bob was a much more creative thinker than I was. When he got back from being at sea, he was fascinated with the puppets. He thought it was a little goofy that I used a crow and a frog for my stories, and he started looking into other puppet ministries.

He checked around and found a puppeteer in San Diego that used gourds for puppets. Her puppets were marionettes (puppets attached to strings). She had a big stage and a lot of people to operate the puppets. It was quite a production. We could see that marionettes required too many people for us to operate, so we decided to use fist puppets. (Fist puppets are the ones that most people are familiar with, because you put your hand into the puppet to operate it.) After we attended one of her workshops on how to make puppets, she put us in touch with a man who had a gourd farm. We went to the gourd farm and picked out gourds from which we would make our puppets. From that point on we were puppeteers.

We started writing scripts and putting music together. Bob built a big stage with powerful lights. It was amazing!

After Bob got out of the Navy, we moved to Texas. Bob felt he was supposed to go to the seminary there, so we bought a home and settled down. But just as Bob was getting admitted to the seminary, he felt that the Lord was telling him we were to go on the road as Kids Crusaders. We had the puppets and all the equipment we needed, so we travelled a long time as Kids Crusaders. It was a lot of fun and was very interesting to see all the many different facets of ministries and elements to our church denomination.

When you work with children, you can be sure amusing things are going to happen; and we certainly had our share.

We had been traveling for several years, and only went home on major holidays like Easter and Christmas, at which time we had a TV station and an oil company lined up to do their parties for the children of their employees. The ministry was still pretty new to us, so we didn't realize that some of our puppets needed to be refurbished.

We had done our routines many times. Bob was the front man and he would get everyone's attention. He would be out in front of everyone saying something like, "We're so glad to see everyone this evening, etc.…" In the meantime, I would be in the puppet stage with a red and blue puppet we had made out of a gourd and a red dust mop. He sort of looked like a Hippy woodpecker. First I would make the puppet peek out of the curtains behind Bob's back.

"Look! Look!" the kids would shout and point to the stage.

Bob would pretend to not know what was going on, and he would turn around real fast to see what they were pointing to. Well, of course, I had pulled the puppet down and then stuck it out the side of the stage.

"It's over there!" they would scream. Bob would run over to that side of the stage. In the meantime, I would poke the puppet out the other side of the stage.

"Now it's over there!" they would scream. Bob would run over to the other side and say, "You guys are just seeing things." In the meantime, He would make his way back to the front of the stage and have his back to the stage curtains. While he had his back turned to the puppet stage, a large, Texas-style flyswatter would come out and swat him over the head; the kids would go crazy. The puppet would show up a few more times, and Bob would try to catch it; but, of course, he never caught the puppet—except for one time.

One night, we had done this so often, that I must have just been distracted, and Bob actually caught the puppet.

"Gotcha!" he cried. And he grabbed the puppet's head.

Now, he wasn't supposed to catch the puppet. When I realized what was happening, in order to get it away from him, I pulled down hard on the stick that the puppet was attached to.

Need I say that we beheaded the puppet in front of all those children? Let me set the stage a little better so you can imagine this: The puppet (which was a gourd) still had its seeds in it and something that looked a lot like sawdust. We had big, bright lights that protruded from the puppet stage so that no shadows would be on the puppets. And in that bright, streaming light, the seeds and the sawdust fell out of the puppet's head, making a very grim scene indeed. The room got very quiet. Bob and I just looked at each other. What should we do now?

All of a sudden the kids started shouting, "Do it again! Do it again!" We didn't do it again, of course, but it was a very memorable moment.

At the next meeting, we were doing the story about the Good Samaritan. We had built a special prop that would hold about four puppets and we could have a really good fight scene when the bandits beat up the good man who was on his way to Jericho. We didn't realize it, but the glue had dried out on one of the puppet's head, and during the fight scene the head came off, flew out of the puppet stage, bounced off the stage, and rolled down the aisle. There was a mob scene as the kids scrambled to catch that head. Once again, all we could do was look at each other and wonder what we should do. But the kids rescued us once again: As the head was returned to us, they all began to chant again: "Do it again! Do it again!"

God gives us memorable moments. ☺

The Bicycles – Becky

I have never been a fan of bicycles for children—at least not for my children. And I did the best I could to keep my children from having any. But if kids want to ride a bike, there is always someone who will let them ride theirs. And such was the case with Becky.

She came in from playing one day and had a bad scrape about the size of a quarter on her leg near her ankle, which, as I recall, came from riding someone else's bike. It was pretty badly scraped, but it didn't look too serious. We cleaned it, put some medicine on it and expected it to go away. But it didn't go away. In fact, it got bigger. We kept cleaning it and putting medicine on it, but then it got as big as a silver dollar. Then it started growing up her leg. It looked like the cells were splitting under the top layer of her skin. We were very concerned, so I took her to a dermatologist. He looked at it and shook his head.

"My wife had the same thing, he said. "It belongs to the School of Medicine. We never did find out what was wrong with her."

Well, that wasn't what I wanted to hear. He gave us a prescription for some medicine, but said it might not work—and it didn't.

Time went by, and the condition was nearly up to her knee.

As it turned out, a very famous evangelist, who has since passed away, was going to be at our church. So I made sure that Becky and I went to his meeting. When the time came for those who needed healing to come forward, Becky and I went forward. I looked to see where the evangelist was standing, and I went to that end of the line. When all the people who needed prayer finally got lined up, the evangelist walked to the opposite end of the line. I was hoping we weren't in trouble with that, but I kind of thought we were.

Now, the denomination that we attended was a Full Gospel, Bible-believing, filled-with-the-Holy Spirit, tongues-talking church. It was not uncommon for people to pass out under the Spirit when they were prayed for. I kid you not, the line was long; and everyone—EVERYONE who got prayed for went out under the Spirit.

Becky was about eight years old, and her eyes got bigger every time someone hit the ground. I could feel the tension rising. When he finally got to us, Becky screamed, turned around, cried, "MAMA!" and held on to me for dear life.

Well, I was there to get my little girl prayed for—and I wasn't leaving that platform until he prayed for her. It was a little awkward, and he grumbled something about people who brought their kids up; but I explained the problem to him about her leg, and he prayed for her. I want you to know that condition on her leg went away—that moment. That was many years ago, and it has never returned.

Even when things are awkward—God is Faithful!

The Bicycles – Rachel

As I stated before, I have never been a fan of bicycles—at least not for *my* children. But we could see that the girls were going to ride bikes whether we bought one or not; so when the neighbors were giving away a perfectly good bike, we took it. The girls were instructed that they were not to ride it without adult supervision or permission. Does that strike you as something that is going to happen? NOT!

We were living in Texas at this juncture, and Bob and I seldom were able to go out to dinner by ourselves; but this one late afternoon all the neighbor kids were outside playing, and we asked the next door neighbors if they would watch the girls while we went out to eat.

They said, "Sure. Have a good time. We'll keep a sharp eye on them."

We had a lovely dinner before it got dark, and we took a nice, leisurely drive home. When we got home the whole neighborhood was in an uproar!

When we pulled into the driveway, the neighbors ran to the car and said, "Rachel's okay!" (You see, this was before cell phones. We had no idea what they were talking about.)

We said, "Okay.....tell us about how she's okay."

"Rachel got run over by a car!"

"Rachel got run over by a car! How did that happen?"

"Yes, but she's okay."

"What happened?"

"Well, the neighbor boy was backing out of the driveway and not looking where he was going. Rachel was *riding her bike* and not watching where she was going. And he ran over her and the bike! We all screamed for him to stop, but he was listening to music and didn't hear us!"

We were speechless. Rachel was nowhere to be seen.

The neighbor said, "We don't know how she escaped being injured, but we were able to pull her and the bike out from under the car!"

Have you ever been in Texas on a hot summer day? The streets are so hot they'll melt the soles off your shoes. How Rachel escaped severe injuries is beyond me—but she didn't even get a burn from the hot blacktop on the street!

They said all Rachel could think of was, "Don't tell my parents I was riding my bike. Don't tell my parents….."

Would it surprise you if I told you we got rid of *that* bicycle *that* day?

God was merciful to us all, both on that day and when Becky had her problem with a bike. Rachel and Becky both grew up to be beautiful ladies and gave us wonderful grandchildren, for which I am very grateful.

Psalm 116:5

Gracious is the Lord, and righteous; yea, our God is merciful.

The Trip to Israel

While we travelled, I was taking ministerial courses and was fascinated with the idea of going to Israel someday. But that seemed like a very far-fetched idea.

One day, as I was studying, I felt that the Lord told me I was going to Israel and that I should buy comfortable, sturdy walking shoes to wear in Israel. I told Bob about it, but he wasn't convinced. So, I started getting ready to go shopping for my shoes.

He said, "Where are you going?"

I said, "I'm going to buy my Israel shoes. Do you want to come and buy yours?"

He just sort of laughed and said, "No, but you go ahead."

I said, "Okay, but if you don't buy your shoes, you won't be able to go." He just laughed and told me to go ahead.

So I went shopping and came home with a pair of shoes that I knew would be very comfortable and sensible, and I put them in the closet so I would have them for my trip.

Bob was always very tolerant of things I did, but I think I was pushing him over the edge on this one. Anyway, within a couple weeks he was invited to interview for a pastoral position in New Mexico. He flew there and talked to the people, and then they wanted to meet me.

He said, "I don't know what's going to happen to your trip to Israel, Jerry; because, I think they are going to want us to pastor their church."

He was right. We got the church and moved to New Mexico.

After we moved there and got settled, I started teaching a Bible class, and we had a good group of people coming.

One Sunday morning a woman stood up and asked if she could say something. Bob said, "Of course."

The woman stood up and this is what she said: "I am going to Israel and I would like to pay Sister Baird's way to go with us. Anyone who enjoys teaching the Bible as much as she does deserves to go."

The trip to Israel was wonderful, but it wasn't just a trip to Israel. On that trip I also went to Turkey.

Now, Turkey is not a country you want to go to if you fear earthquakes. And I had really bad earthquake nerves.

In July 1952, California had a really bad earthquake. It was referred to as the "Tehachapi Earthquake." Even though we lived 131 miles from the epicenter, it was terrifying. The roar alone was terrifying, and I just couldn't stop thinking about it. Today we would have had therapists or counselors who could have helped those who were traumatized; but there wasn't any such thing in 1952.

For years I watched to see if lamps were swinging, if doors were moving. My life was consumed with watching for earthquakes—even imagined earthquakes. But I wasn't thinking about earthquakes when I went on that trip. The first place we went was Turkey. In Turkey are the sites of the seven churches written to in the book of Revelation in the Bible. It is also a country that has bad earthquakes.

As part of that trip and going to see the site of the seven churches, we went to

Cappadocia, Turkey, to see the caves and the rock houses. Then the cruise director announced that we would be able to visit the underground cites below Derinkuyu, Turkey. The first one they planned to see went underground as far as seven stories.

I was okay with this until we started going underground, and then I just couldn't do it. I tried to enter several times, and I just had to back out. I was chocking with fear of an earthquake that would bury all of us under seven stories of tunnels. The director was not the least bit happy with me and told me to stay near the bus driver, and that it was dangerous for me to be there alone. So I stayed above ground. It turned out to be a lot of fun. I had a polaroid camera and I took pictures of kids and women. Shop owners wanted their pictures taken in front of their stores, and they gave me gifts in return.

But the longer the group stayed underground, the more I realized that I had allowed fear to rob me. The Lord had not only paid my way to Turkey, He had paid my way home. And I had missed out on seeing the underground city.

Soon the group returned and everyone was very excited. The Director had said they could go to another underground city! You can be sure I went with them this time. And, not only that, I never suffered from fear of earthquakes again. I was healed! I'm not saying that I wouldn't be frightened if we had another big one, but I will never again live in the terrible "anticipation" of an earthquake.

Need I say more? The Lord had not only given me the desire of my heart, He had healed me from a morbid fear of earthquakes.

Our New House

We traveled a lot when our girls were young, but there came a time when we quit traveling and moved to California. At first we lived with relatives. It was not a fun time. When I would drive down the streets to go shopping or get gas or whatever, I would think, "There are so many houses here. Isn't there just one of these houses that I can call mine?"

Bob and I both got jobs and ultimately moved into a small house which we rented. Many of the houses in California don't have the same type of insulating that ones in other states have, and this rental apparently had no insulating at all. In the winter, it was so cold inside that house we would nearly freeze to death. Even with the heat on, we might as well have been living outside on the street. When it rained, it wasn't that the roof leaked, because it didn't—but the walls did! The rain would literally come in the walls and mold was forming in the closets.

Finally we had to come to grips with the realization that we needed to buy our own house. Now, I don't know how much you know about the housing market in California, but that isn't just something you decide to do and then walk out and do it—unless you have LOTS OF MONEY! It is EXPENSIVE to live in California! I wanted for us to have our own home, but it seemed so impossible. I had been on my job less than a year, and we had no money in the bank. The possibilities weren't very promising. But, true to form, we decided to find a real estate agent and see what we could do.

The first hurdle we had to jump was being qualified for a loan. The second hurdle was trying to find a house we could afford. We looked at several houses—which were waaaay out of our price range. Then the real estate agent said that she knew of a "fixer-upper" on the market that she thought we would be interested in. It had been on the market for quite a while and no one was interested, but it was the size we wanted. The neighborhood was just about where we wanted to locate, so we said, "Let's have a look."

Now, we were expecting to see a real dump. The agent said every time she tried to show it, when they would pull up in front of the house, the clients would say, "Just keep on driving." So you can only imagine what was going through our minds. Well, we visited the fixer-upper and it was exactly what we wanted. It was a little dirty, the carpets had big black spots on them, but, hopefully, we could get new carpets. The inside walls were yellow (a very ugly yellow—but they could be painted), and the lawn hadn't been mowed, seemingly, since the current residents moved in (We could mow the lawn.); but we would worry about all that later. So we made an offer. Bob had been in the military, so we decided to go with a VA, no-down loan (mainly because we had no down). As soon as we put our offer in, an investor came in over the top of our offer and said he would pay $5,000.00 more than what she was asking. Unbelievable as it sounds, the seller wanted a family to live in the house and didn't want to sell to an investor, so she asked us for $500 in "earnest" money, "good faith" money! Well, I told the agent as "earnestly" as I could that I didn't have $500. Not only that, I didn't have the "good faith" that I was going to get the "earnest" money. The agent said, "Oh, just write them a check!" I couldn't believe my ears!

"Please understand," I said as plainly as I could, "I don't have $500 in the bank to cover that check."

"Oh," she said, "they're not going to cash it. It's just going to sit in an escrow account until escrow closes. You can take care of it then." (In California, when you buy a house, you go through an intermediary third party called "Escrow." They hold all monies and contracts to keep everyone honest.)

"Are you sure no one is going to cash that check?" I had visions of my face being splashed on TV for writing hot checks: I could see the caption: "MINISTER'S WIFE WRITES HOT CHECK TO BUY HOUSE!"

"Positive.   That   check   isn't   going anywhere!" the real estate agent assured me.

So the Bairds went into escrow.   It seemed like it took an eternity for that escrow to close; but one day it did close and it was time to settle up for the $500 check. I scratched the money together, somehow; but, instead of _US_ having to pay _THEM_ $500—THEY OWED US $500! I said, "How did that happen?" The agent just shrugged her shoulders and said, "It just works like that sometimes."

We were more than happy to accept the $500 windfall; because now we had their $500 and our $500. We had to paint, paper, hang curtains and lay new rugs—all with $1,000!

At this late date, I can't quite recall where a man selling carpet came from, but he had very nice carpeting that he was selling very cheaply (and it included the padding for under the carpet). We jumped at his offer. I don't ever want to know where he got that carpeting and padding. All I know is that we were able to paint and paper, put up curtains, and lay carpeting in the three bedrooms and the hallway with that $500—plus the $500 that I had scratched together. There was even enough for Bob to buy varnish to refinish the front room floor.

God had given me the desire of my heart—with money to spare!

It was a nice house. It had good paint on the outside, so we just hosed the dirt off the outside walls and painted the trim and the front door. Bob made beautiful hanging baskets for the front porch and planted lovely flowers all around the front and sides of the house. We even got an award from the city for most-improved house. Soon we learned that the house had a very interesting story to go along with it. It happened that the author Ray Bradbury was the original owner. So, over the years while we lived there, the neighbors regaled us with Bradbury stories.

After we had lived there a number of years, we almost lost the house and our car. I didn't know what to do. I just couldn't meet all our bills. That was a real low point for us financially. We were both working, but the money just didn't stretch far enough. I was so worried.

Out of the blue, a man called and wanted to know if we wanted to refinance the house. I said, "No, I don't think so." Refinancing was something I didn't really understand, and besides, I didn't want to answer all the bank's questions. But he was persistent, and he kept calling. We were coming closer and closer to losing the house—and our car! Finally the man asked me, "Why won't you refinance? I can lower your payments by about $400 a month." Finally, I said, "Our credit is bad. I haven't been able to keep up with the bills. Anyway, they're going to ask a lot of embarrassing questions and probably deny our credit in the end. And, besides, I don't have the money to pay the escrow charges!"

He said, "If you didn't have to answer the embarrassing questions and not pay the escrow payments, would you refinance if I could get your house payment lowered by at least $400 a month. Finally, I said, "yes." So I agreed to refinance and the house went into escrow. Soon it was time to sign the papers. I read them all, and, sure enough, the payments were lowered by at least $400. At this point in time, I can't remember the exact amount, but it was substantial. So, I went to the escrow company to sign the papers and the woman at the escrow wanted money—a lot of money. I said, "I was told I didn't have to pay anything." She said, "You must have misunderstood." I said, "I didn't misunderstand anything." And with that I got up and started to walk out.

"Wait a minute," she called out. "I need to make a phone call." So she called the man who had been calling me. The man on the phone told her, "Jerry is exactly right." With that, I got an affordable loan on the house and with greatly reduced payment, I didn't have to answer any embarrassing questions, I didn't have to pay any escrow fees. I didn't have to pay a dime! My payment was lowered about $400 a month, and I didn't lose the house, and with the lower house payment, we didn't lose the car. I never met that man or ever laid eyes on him. But, God bless him! He worked a miracle for us, and **God gave me the desire of my heart by allowing us to keep the house and the car.**

Like a lot of people, in spite of all God had done for us, I began to feel sorry for myself, and I became very unhappy with the house. It just didn't seem as nice as other people's houses, or the houses down the street. Those people had swimming pools, and better cars; everything we had just seemed old and tired and outdated. I began to wish I had something better.

In that particular year, California had a very cold winter. The bitterly cold temperature was referred to as the Arctic Blast (or words to that effect). Anyway, it was really cold. California had begun to get a lot of migrant, homeless people; and I began wondering how the homeless people were doing in this weather. The Orange County Mission wasn't very far from our house, so I went through the closets and gathered up every coat and sweater that I knew hadn't been worn for years (some with the price tags still on them), put them in big leaf sacks and took them to the mission (The mission has since moved to a different location where it is now located).

As I pulled up in front of the mission, I could see many people lying in closed store fronts. They were all huddled up in blankets on the cold, hard cement, and I was afraid to get out of the car. As I looked at those people, every eye was on me and my car. I decided to wait until someone came by before I got out of the car. Soon a car pulled up behind me. I hid my purse in the car, grabbed my leaf bags which were filled with warm wraps, locked the car, and bolted for the front door of the mission. As I did, a man got in step with me and asked me to give him the bags. He wanted to know if I had clothes in the bags, and he said the people inside the mission wouldn't give them the clothing. About that time, someone got in step with the man that got in step with me, and said, "Leave her alone." I didn't know who that was, but I was mighty glad he was there.

When I got inside, the first man was still in step with me, and I told the man at the front desk what had been said to me. He said, "He's right. So I'll tell you how it works. Before we give anyone any clothing, we make them come in and take a shower. Then we clothe them from the skin out with clean clothing, and that includes warm clothing like coats and sweaters." And then he went into detail about how the clothing distribution worked. "This fella here just wants to take the things you have and trade them for drugs." That satisfied me. I handed over the bags and headed for my car.

When I got back into my car, the whole world looked different to me. My car looked better and newer. It even seemed to run better. I was thankful to even have a car and to be able to put gas into it. And when I got home and pulled up in front of my house, I will never forget how huge and beautiful it looked to me. I never complained or felt bad about that house again. To me it was a mansion. **God had changed my perspective and had given me the desire of my heart.**

We lived there a long time. Bob and I both eventually got jobs in aerospace and worked there quite a while. Bob really wanted to get back into the ministry and was writing sermons when, all of a sudden, aerospace shut down and started laying people off. We both lost our jobs!

The place where I worked was so big that we had company busses that would carry us from building to building. As this was all going on, I was riding on one of the company busses and I started talking to the woman sitting next to me. She was in shock. She had received her pink slip notifying her that her job was terminated. She said, "My whole family works in aerospace. I don't know what we will do. None of us have ever worked anywhere else!"

The layoffs came in waves, and I lost my job during the third wave. This was really serious, because Bob lost his job in the fourth wave and we were going to have to sell our house. The problem with selling the house was that thousands of people in our area had to sell their house because of the RIF (Reduction in Force), and so our house was just one among thousands that suddenly flooded the housing market. But out of all the thousands of houses that were on the market, our house sold, and we made a good profit. **God took care of us, and from there we went back into the ministry. God gave Bob the desire of his heart.**

We serve a risen savior! He is our High Priest who can be moved by our infirmities.

> [15] For we have not an high priest which cannot be touched with the feeling of our infirmities; but was in all points tempted like as we are, yet without sin.
>
> [16] Let us therefore come boldly unto the throne of grace, that we may obtain mercy, and find grace to help in time of need. Hebrews 4:15-16 (KJV)

The Flood

After losing our jobs in aerospace, we were accepted as pastors of a church in Indiana. We eventually bought an old, two-story house and did some renovating to it. We loved that house. It reminded us of Narnia (from "The Chronicles of Narnia" by C. S. Lewis). It was situated at the edge of a beautiful state park. In autumn the entire area becomes a blaze of color and is stunning. We had a hedge at the back of the house that, in autumn, was so red it almost looked like it was on fire. The leaves on the trees up and down the streets were bright and shiny reds, burgundies, golds, yellows; just imagine the most glorious fall colors you can envision. When springtime came it was like the earth had new birth. There were exotic weeping redbud trees that ranged in shades from pink to lavender; azalea shrubs of white and many shades of red, pink, and lavender; rhodo-dendrons; great white flowering bushes six to seven feet tall and full of flowers. The bushes were filled with flowers, and the colors were unimaginably beautiful.

We were very happy there and planned to live there the rest of our lives. Our house sat on two lots. The front of the house faced one street, and the back of the house faced the next street over. Bob always liked to work in the yard. It was so big it took him two days to mow. For his birthday, I hired a man to come in and disc up a large plot so Bob could plant a garden. He was thrilled with that.

In the meantime, my husband's sister and her husband lived in Ohio and pastored a church there. For some reason (I can't remember why), Bob's brother-in-law had been talking to the District Superintendent in Ohio about us. A church came open, and the superintendent wanted Bob and me to pastor that church. We talked about it, but we didn't really want to leave the church we were in, so we said no.

Time went by. The superintendent called us again. He said, "I really feel like you are the people to pastor this church." We said no again. We liked it where we were. So Bob's brother-in-law called and said, "Why don't you just come to Ohio for a visit and see the church and see how you feel about it?" So we said we would come to visit them, and during the visit we could look at the church. Well, the "church" did not have its own building. Rather, they were renting space from a church of another denomination that was an active church, and we would have to have our meetings at an "off" time. I dug my heels in and said no. "I don't want to go there." So we went back to Indiana and thought we had heard the last of that.

After we got back from that trip, the lawn needed to be mowed. One of the men from our church came over for a visit and saw Bob mowing the lawn. He said, "Brother Baird doesn't need to be mowing a lawn for two days. I'm going to go get my rider mower and mow it for him."

So Bob came in the house and told me about it. I said, "Tell him to be sure to pick up all the cut grass so we don't have a bunch of dead grass lying in the yard." He said okay, and we didn't think any more about it.

That night Bob and I were lying in bed listening to a rain storm. Bob said, "That's a pretty good storm." I said, "Yep, it sounds like it's right overhead." Then the storm sounded like it was letting up and going away. But, wait a minute; It's back. Now it's going away. No, it's coming back. It rained like that all night.

Finally, we decided we had better get up and see what was going on. And what was going on was really a jaw-dropper. Our house sat up high on a knoll, and our backyard had a slope of

17-feet from the front of our house to the lowest spot in the backyard. So to drive out of the backyard, we drove *up* to the next street. This made our property sort of like a bowl back there, and we had a lake in our bowl!   Our garage, Bob's garden, and both of our cars were under water. We ran to the front of the house to see what was happening there. The street in front of the house was like a cascading waterfall.

I had often wondered what I would try to save in an emergency.   Well, I grabbed our pictures and our bibles and ran upstairs with them. That was it!

In all of its history, that town had never had a flood: but we were in the middle of a flood! The rock query at the edge of town had filled up with water, and the rest of the water was headed our way. This was going to be a catastrophe!

Bob and I stood in the back door of our house and watched the rain fall and the water rise. We had a basement; it was no doubt full of water by now, because the seventeen-foot slope in the back yard was now full of water, and the flood waters were now backing up to the house; it was within six inches of coming in the house. As we stood there, we knew that if it didn't stop raining like—right now--our house would be ruined. And we didn't even know at that point how we could get out of the house. People were now being taken out of their houses in boats and canoes. As we stood there watching the rain come down and the water coming up, I said, "Bob, if it's really God's will for us to go to Ohio, I will go if the Lord will stop the rain." So we joined hands, prayed and told God we would go to Ohio if that was His will. The rain stopped that instant and the flood water immediately began to go down! It was as if someone had turned the spout off and pulled the plug!

We were dumbfounded. But we had nevertheless cut a deal with the Lord and we had to keep our commitment. So, as soon as we could, we called the district superintendent in Ohio and told him we would move to Ohio and take the church if it was still available.

After the water went down (and it went down fast), we got out to see what damage had been done. It took a while (like days), but when we were able to get into the basement, we saw several things: The man that mowed the lawn did not pick up the cut grass and it had all funneled into the basement—which now looked like it needed a shave because the cut grass was stuck all over the walls. Also, we could see where the water stopped: it was within three inches of the flooring.

This was not exactly a desire of my heart, but it was definitely God working in a very positive way in our life. That turn of events followed us all the rest of our lives.

We took the church in Ohio, and we were blessed in many ways there, also. Someday I will write a sequel to this book and tell you about the adventures in Ohio. For now, I would like to tell you about a few more ways the Lord gave me the desires of my heart or met a deep need.

The Surgery

Shortly before we resigned the church in Ohio, we attended an evangelistic meeting that was being held by an evangelist whose meetings we had attended before we ever moved to Ohio. He wasn't anyone we knew personally, we just liked his ministry. So we managed to get in on the last evening of his meeting.

During that meeting, he called my husband out of the audience and said he wanted to pray for him. He asked him if he was a minister, and Bob said yes. He said, "Are you leaving your church?"

Now, we had plans to resign, but we hadn't told anyone, so this was an "awkward" moment; it was "awkward" because, members of our congregation were there in attendance at that meeting. I don't remember exactly how Bob answered that, but the evangelist moved on with some prophecies about Bob's future.

Then he turned and pointed to me. "Is that your wife?" he asked.

Now, I am not someone that gets called out in that type of meeting. I could walk in half dead and not be noticed. But I was noticed that night.

"Would you come up here, Darlin'?" the evangelist drawled. "The Lord has something to say to you."

Bob knew how uncomfortable that made me and he sort of laughed. Neither one of us knew what to expect, especially since he had just outed our plans to leave the church. When I got up there, the evangelist began to speak.

He said, "You're going to have some surgery in your female parts, and **you're going to feel better than you've felt in a long time."**

Now, I was really getting nervous, because I felt just fine and wasn't having any problems. He continued: **"But you're not even going to get to brag about the scar**!"

I thought, "Okay. Can I sit down now?" But he had a few more things to say about a future ministry for me, and then he appeared to be finished, and I started to go back to my seat.

Then he said, "No, don't leave, Darlin'. The Lord has more to say." He turned around and motioned to some of the ladies. "Could one of you ladies come up here and help me?" One of the ladies of the church promptly stepped to my side.

"I want you to put your hands over her breast area while I pray for her." At that point he began to curse cancer, and he prayed for quite a while. Then he told me I could return to my seat, and he commenced with the rest of the service.

Bob and I didn't talk much about it, but I wasn't sick, and no one in my family had cancer. I just couldn't imagine why the evangelist did that. So I just brushed it off as him speaking "evangelistically." However, I did call the church and asked for a tape of that meeting, which they sent to me.

Time passed. We resigned from our church and returned to California. I got a job as an office manager and life went on.

After I had worked for about a year, I suddenly developed a terrific pain in my back—at least, I thought it was in my back. I went to a chiropractor—because it was in my back. I went for a number of treatments, but I began to develop other symptoms and the pain got worse. So I went to a general practitioner. When I described my symptoms, he didn't even bother to examine me. He said he could tell by my symptoms that I should meet with the gynecologist and that he would put in an order for me to make an appointment at the GYN department.

The gynecologist examined me, told me to get dressed and then come into his office. Okay, that was kind of scary. And this is what he said: You need to have a double surgery. Your uterus has fallen and it tore your bladder." (That's where all the back pain was coming from.) He was quite descriptive of what would happen if I put the surgery off. I needed surgery immediately. But he finished with these words: **"But you're not even going to get to brag about the scar**!"

I said, "What did you say?"

He repeated what he said: **"You're not even going to get to brag about the scar!** We have a new procedure called laparoscopy. We don't do the abdominal surgery with the big abdominal incision any more. With laparoscopy you will only have some very small incision marks which won't even be visible if you wear a bathing suit. So you won't even have a scar to brag about!" This is what the evangelist had said! Then the doctor said, **"You're going to feel better than you've felt in a long time!"**

I said, "Let's make the appointment right now." I knew I was in God's hands and that He had his prophet tell me about it long before I needed it.

I had a nine-week recovery period and lost a lot of weight in the process. I felt great. In fact, **I felt better than I had felt in a long time,** just like the evangelist had prophesied. I had a problem and I didn't even know it!

As you can imagine, we talked about that prophecy a lot, but there was also the prophecy about breast cancer. Well, I was happy enough to get through this surgery. I wasn't going to push my luck for any more.

I couldn't drive for nine weeks, so my daughter drove me back and forth to the doctor visits.

On one of those trips, I told Rachel, "I have the attention of all these doctors while I'm recovering. I'm going to ask them to give me some hormones. I'm hot all the time and I think that will put a stop to it.

So on my next trip to the doctor, I told him I wanted some hormones. He said, "What for?" So I explained that I was like in continual hot-flash mode, and I wanted something to take care of it.

His next question was, "How long has it been since you had a mammogram?" He could tell by the blank look I gave him that I hadn't had one.

He said, "No mammogram, no hormones."

Okay, I knew when I was whipped. "Write out a request form and I will get it done."

The day came for the mammogram. I still wasn't driving, so Rachel and I went to get the mammogram.

Everything was going pretty good. The technician took all the pictures and asked me to wait while she took them to the doctor. Pretty soon she came back and said, "The doctor would like to see more pictures of your right breast." That was not what I was expecting, but we took some more pictures. The technician said I could get dressed and that they would be getting in touch with me about the results. She said not to worry, that many woman have to have extra pictures taken and that chances were that it was nothing.

Before I could get home, the doctor who read the mammogram had called the gynecologist, who, in turn, called my husband. By the time I got there, Bob was worried out of his mind, and he had to tell me I had cancer. He just looked at me and said, "The doctor wants you to call him. You have breast cancer."

At first, it was just too horrible to have someone say my name and the word "cancer" in the same sentence. I just looked at him. The thought of picking up the phone and making that call was like writing my own death sentence. I wanted to reason with myself and say, "If I don't call, it won't be true."

But I did call, and it was true, and we started through the process of having a biopsy. **Then I remembered the second part of the prophecy.** The evangelist had cursed cancer. I listened to the tape. Yep, that's what he did: he CURSED cancer. So this started a round of doctor visits.

First I went to the doctor who was going to perform the surgery, and he explained that the cancer was "in situ." That means that the cancer was "in the natural or original position or place. It was an **in situ cancer** confined to the breast duct." My cancer was confined to the breast duct and they had removed all of it! And this cancer surgeon wanted to do a mastectomy!

I said, "Didn't you just say you got all of it?" The answer to that question was yes. My mother-in-law and father-in-law had both died of cancer, and I began asking him a lot of questions.

His response to my questions was this: "Since you seem to know something about cancer, I'm going to recommend that you talk to the oncologist."

The appointment was made for me to see the oncologist, and I began to look up breast cancer on the Internet. It was very informative and I was ready to talk to another doctor. Bob and Rachel went with me.

The oncologist was very much to the point and right up front recommended that I have a mastectomy and that he wanted to take some lymph nodes from under my arm and do chemo therapy.

My response was that I had been doing research on breast cancer and felt that women who had radiation treatments fared better than women who had chemo. At which point, Bob and Rachel nearly fainted and told me not to tell the doctor what to do.

"What *research* have *you* done?" he asked. He was very condescending. I informed him that I had read every case I could find on the Internet and that I wasn't having any lymph nodes removed and I wasn't having chemo.

"Well," he said, "since you have done your "*research,*" I am going to recommend that you see the radiologist." Bob and Rachel could not believe their ears.

Next, Bob and I went to the radiologist. And this is what the radiologist said: "I am an expert in reading x-rays, and I can tell you that you have no need for anyone to do any more cutting on you. I can't tell you 100% that this cancer will never come back, but I can tell you that I am 99.9% sure that it will never come back. We will set up a schedule for your treatments."

That was many years ago. The cancer never came back. But I can assure you, were it not for the evangelist and his prophetic message, I could have never been that brave.

God is good. He directs our path.

The Chair and the Rug

I've always loved to look at architectural magazines and see beautiful houses and how they are furnished.   In this particular period of time, every architectural magazine I picked up, no matter what the design of the home was, and no matter how the house was furnished, i.e. contemporary, modern, traditional, West Coast Living, you name it, there was one chair that was always in the picture: It was a beautiful accent chair upholstered with fabric that had a black-and-white zebra design, and with arms, legs and backboard of black enamel.   I loved that chair.   But, every time I checked the price on it, it was always $500—or more.   I loved it, but I didn't love it $500 worth.   So I would enjoy looking at it, but I didn't think I would ever own it.

One day, I was out doing my chores, i.e., grocery shopping, and anything that was on my list to do that day.   All of a sudden I felt that I should go into a particular store that I didn't normally shop in.   Those kinds of hunches or leadings always lead me to interesting things or experiences, so I drove to the shopping center where I knew one of those stores was and decided to take a quick run around the store to see what was there. And what was there stopped me dead in my tracks. When I came to the area that had furniture, there was the zebra chair! And it wasn't $500; it was $150. I just stood there and stared at it! Finally, I called my husband.

"Bob, I saw a chair I want to buy, but it costs $150. Would you like for me to pick you up so you can see it?"

He didn't even have to think about it. He said, "Jerry, in all the years we've been married, I have never known you to buy a chair. That must be some kind of a chair. Come and get me."

So I drove back home to get him. I was very anxious to get back to the store, as I certain that the entire world knew the chair was there and that they would be lined up to purchase theirs.

Thankfully, word hadn't filtered out to the rest of the world while I was gone, and the chair was still there.

Bob loved it. He said, "Do they have more? Let's buy several." Well, I didn't want several; I just wanted that one chair, so I proudly bought my zebra chair and put it in my living room.

I also had been saving money to buy a carpet for the front room, and it couldn't be just any carpet: it had to be special. We had a new grandson, and I wanted his visits to our house to be special. This had to be a carpet that he would identify with.

Finally, I felt I had saved up enough money and told Bob it was time to go carpet shopping. I didn't know exactly what I was looking for; I just knew I would recognize it when I saw it. So we looked and looked, but we didn't find anything we liked. We were about to go home when I remembered a yardage store that I liked to trade in that also had carpeting. We decided it would be the last stop for the day.

That store had every kind of rug imaginable, but nothing that grabbed my attention. We were about to leave when Bob noticed they had a lot of rugs on sale in the back of the store. I was looking for a 9' X 12' rug, and nothing seemed to be what I would want in the front room (I had looked at too many architectural magazines.). One of the clerks came back to help us. He opened up a carpet that was 7' x 10' and it had the design of giraffe skin. It was beautiful, and I loved it; but it was too short all the way around. I thought about it. I really liked it and thought it might fit in well, so I said I would take it. It cost about $500, and the clerks started taking it down from the rack; but then they stopped.

"We have this same rug in 9' X 12' and we're clearing it out for $175. Could you use it in 9' X 12'?"

"Yes! 9' X 12' is what I was looking for. Is there anything wrong with it? Is it a second? Is it the exact same rug as the 7' X 10'?"

"It's the exact same rug. We're just clearing it out. Would you like to see it? Of course I wanted to see it, and it was everything I could hope for. It was perfect!

We bought padding for it, and it was a wonderful rug that I always loved.

God led me to the two items I really loved, saw to it that I got exactly what I wanted, and I got much enjoyment out of them both. He gave me the desires of my heart.

Appendicitis and a Hernia

Bob and I were married 44 years before he went to be with the Lord.

I had always viewed myself as being the strong one in the family. I had worked for an adult daycare center for about six years, and two things we all learned: 1.) Very few things in life prepare you for what happens when you age; and 2.) When the person who is being cared for passes away, the caregiver frequently has a bevy of health problems.

A year had passed since Bob left us. I had lost 80 pounds, and was congratulating myself on the fact that I hadn't had any adverse health problems. On the particular day that I was congratulating myself, my stomach was a little upset. I made some soup and decided I would feel better if I could just lie down. So I went upstairs to go to bed.

Just as my feet got on the landing of the second floor, I was struck with the most horrible pain.   It hurt so bad my whole world turned orange.   The only thing I could think of was: 1.) I was by myself, and 2.) I was on the second floor and didn't know how I was going to get downstairs to get help.

All I could do was pray that someone would call me.   At that moment, the phone rang. By that time I was in the bedroom. I had put my phone on the bed, but it was covered up by the sheets and I was in so much pain I couldn't find it. Then, whoever called hung up.

I said, "Lord, please have them call me on the landline."

The landline rang.   It was Rachel.   She said, "Mom, are you okay?"

I said, "No, I'm in terrible pain."

As it happened, she was with her husband's aunt—who just happened to be a nurse.

They were all getting ready to go somewhere, but the aunt thought it sounded like appendicitis, so Rachel told them all to go ahead, and she headed for my house. She called my sister. She and her husband were headed in the direction of my house, so they came, too. When they all got there, I was still upstairs, because I couldn't navigate the stairs with all the pain.

They called an ambulance and helped me get down the stairs.

If you can believe it, when the ambulance guys got there, they thought I was having gas pains. I assured them these were not gas pains. They took me to the hospital where the doctors said my appendix had ruptured. I survived that, thankfully.

Rachel was very intuitive about my health and helped me through the appendicitis, pneumonia, and many other things, one of which was a hernia.

Several years after I had healed from the appendicitis, Becky found a wonderful island that she wanted us all to visit just off the East Coast near Savannah, Georgia, called Jekyll Island. It had a lot of history and we thought it would be a very cool place to spend Thanksgiving.

I left California on Thanksgiving eve, flew five hours to Atlanta, Georgia, met up with Becky and family, and we drove five and one-half hours to Savannah, Georgia, then another hour and a half to Jekyll Island.

While we were there, we had lunch at the Jekyll Island Club, a private club which was founded in 1886. The membership of the club included the world's wealthiest families such as the Morgans, Rockefellers, and the Vanderbilts. It was really a great trip, but I had not allowed a lot of time to go there, so we headed back to Georgia so I could catch my plane back to California and be back at work on Monday morning.

The trip was great but a little too strenuous for me. By the time I got off the plane and got into the car with Rachel in California, I wasn't feeling very well.

By the time we got to Huntington Beach, I was starting to feel some pain. I couldn't eat and started feeling very nauseous and started vomiting. Eric and Rachel had some time constraints. I didn't want to go to the local Emergency Room, so Rachel drove me back to Laguna Woods, and I went to the ER there. Bottom line: I had a hernia and they had to operate right away. I got the same doctor that did the appendectomy, and I survived that, also.

God wasn't ready to take me home yet.

The Trip to Hawaii

At the beginning of this book I quoted **Psalm 37:4:** *Delight thyself also in the LORD: and he shall give thee the desires of thine heart.* And you can see how the Lord has blessed me with that scripture throughout the years.

Some years later I was checking out notations in my Thompson Chain Bible and saw that Psalm 37:4 had the reference **Isaiah 58:14**, so I turned to it. This is what it said:

Then shalt thou delight thyself in the LORD; ***and I will cause thee to ride upon the high places of the earth, and feed thee with the heritage of Jacob thy father****: for the mouth of the LORD hath spoken it.*

I was really struck by the words: "**and I will cause thee to ride upon the high places of the earth, and feed thee with the heritage of Jacob thy father:**"

I had to think about that. It surely couldn't apply to *me*. I was born a Gentile—not a Jew. Jacob was not even remotely my father. The heritage couldn't be mine.

But the Lord began to deal with me and began to point out that I was born again in Christ, and therefore, I am Christ's. What could that mean? So I looked it up.

And in Christ, according to: **Galatians 3:28, 29: There is neither Jew nor Greek, there is neither bond nor free, there is neither male nor female: for ye are all one in Christ. And if ye be Christ's, <u>then are ye Abraham's seed,</u> <u>and heir according to the promise.</u>**

Okay, now He had my attention. Even Christ took on the seed of Abraham! And Jacob was in the line of Abraham. Being born again into the bloodline of Christ, I was not only an heir—I was a double heir!

Hebrews 1:16: *For verily he (Jesus) took not on him the nature of angels; but he took on him the seed of Abraham.*

Hebrews 1:4: <u>Being made so much better than the angels, as He hath by inheritance obtained a more excellent name than they</u>.

I typed this into my prayer and praise list, but I just couldn't see how this was going to apply to me. And, even though I didn't understand how it was going to apply to my life, it excited me and I made everyone in earshot listen to me when I recited those scriptures.

One day, I got a phone call (it might have been a text) from my daughter Becky. She said, "How would you like to go to Hawaii? I'll pay your way!"

HAWAII! I had *ALWAYS* wanted to go to Hawaii. Bob and I had tried to book meetings there. Unfortunately, so had the rest of the evangelistic world; so, we just couldn't make that one work.

I did not have to think this one through for one second. Yes! I definitely wanted to go to Hawaii, and she was paying my way! YES, YES!!

We didn't just go to Hawaii; we went to Kauai, the most distant of the islands. This island has not been commercialized to the extent that the other Hawaiian Islands have been. It is very pristine and you really get the feeling that you are on a "Hawaiian" island.

Becky had rented a beautiful house that was located near the bottom of a long and winding road. It was very private and sat about

100 feet from the ocean. It was built up on stilts, because the ocean frequently floods there.

I had my own room with a TV. It was great! One night, however, I was watching TV (It was about 2:00 a.m.). The windows had those bamboo shades that you can roll up or down, depending on how much sun or privacy you want. Now, those bamboo shades don't *exactly* cover the entire window, so if someone wanted to peek in the windows, they could do so—easily.

Well, I was sitting there, secure in the thought that no one was around for quite a space, when I heard what sounded like claws scrambling on the stairway and deck outside my window. Then, I heard the deepest growl I'd ever heard UP CLOSE—and it was just outside my window, which was about six feet from me— and the window was open! There was a screen on the window, but I wasn't taking much comfort in that.

Did I mention that our cell phones didn't work in that location?

I have heart palpitations from time to time, but I wasn't concerned with whether my heart would start fluttering at that moment: I was more concerned with whether my heart was going to *stop beating* at that moment.

What was that growl coming from? It sounded like something very, very big—like BIG FOOT! DID BIG FOOT LIVE ON KAUAI?!

Well, it took all the courage I could muster up, but I managed to turn the TV and the lights off. I just sat there—afraid to move. I finally inched my way into the living room, which was just outside my bedroom door. It had big sliding windows, so I slowly walked up to the windows to see if I could see anything—which I hoped I couldn't. It didn't look like anyone else woke up, so I finally just decided that I had stayed up too late, got too tired and jumpy, and mistook a plane flying over—or something—for Big Foot. So I went to bed and went to sleep.

The next morning I asked Becky if she heard anything the night before. She said, "What did you hear?" So I told her.

She just laughed and said they had wondered if I had heard anything, but that my lights were out, so they thought I was asleep.

It appears that wild dogs were chasing a wild boar, and they all ran up the stairs and across the deck and back down again at our house. I don't know whether I heard the wild boar or one of the wild dogs. The next morning my son-in-law Eric was taking the trash out and some more wild dogs were chasing a wild boar and they ran right by him.

The landlord, who was in a house nearby, said that he had seen as many as a dozen wild boars in their yard, and that if we saw any barbequing going on, it was probably a wild boar that someone caught, as there was no law against catching and eating them.

Well, we all had a great time, and as we were flying back to California, we were flying past the curve of the earth that contained the Aleutian Islands, and I realized that I was riding upon the **"high places of the earth"** and that I would do so again many times before Time surrendered me and I met my Amazing Maker.

Once again, He had given me the desires of my heart.

Psalm 85:9-13 says:

*¹⁰ **Mercy and truth are met together; righteousness and peace have kissed each other.***
¹¹ Truth shall spring out of the earth; and righteousness shall look down from heaven.
¹² Yea, the Lord shall give that which is good; and our land shall yield her increase.
¹³ Righteousness shall go before him; and shall set us in the way of his steps.

I am very blessed to have the wonderful daughters I have.

God blessed me when he sent me Bob. He has been gone many years now. He was handsome and funny and smart and a great companion. He gave me beautiful daughters. They, in turn, have given me two wonderful sons-in-law and three wonderfully sweet, handsome, and smart grandsons. They all bless my life.

Each of these experiences have shaped our lives in various and sundry ways.

There is much more that I could write, but I will stop for now. My purpose is not to bore you with my life story, but to impress on you that even the worst or smallest of events can carry a huge blessing.

We have all grown up in a world where we see all problems solved in thirty minutes on TV (Twenty minutes if you subtract the commercials). So we want answers to all our problems right away. But real life isn't that way. God does things for us in His own time and His own way, and that usually is longer than 30 minutes to an hour.

We get so attached to people, things and routines. We don't want to lose anything or anyone. We don't want anything to change.

But change brings new life—and new life comes from God. Rejoice! God works and exists in every phase of our life.

*And we know that **all things work together** for good to them that love God, to them who are the called according to his purpose. Romans 8:28*

*But let all those that put their trust in thee **rejoice**: let them ever shout for joy, because thou defendest them: let them also that love thy name be joyful in thee.*

Psalm 5:11

Jerry Baird

About the Author

Jerry Baird earned a BS degree in Business Administration at California State University in Long Beach (CSULB), and an AA degree in Business Administration at Long Beach Community College. While in college, she took a writing course and her love for writing was launched.

She has written, produced and performed plays; had an essay published in the Spanish-Portuguese Department publication El Alba at CSUB; received a special award for poetry in The American Collegiate Poets—Fall Concourse 1983; and also wrote, directed, produced and edited volunteer TV programs for several years at DATV, Channel 22, in Dayton, Ohio.

Jerry now pursues writing full time.

Other books written by the author are:

Daughters of Eve
Grave Walkers
Bob's Vision of Heaven